A Frank Conversation with Today's Youth

Practical suggestions and inspirational
insights for some problems of youths

Pearline James

WESTBOW
PRESS®
A DIVISION OF THOMAS NELSON
& ZONDERVAN

WestBow Press books may be ordered through booksellers or by contacting:

WestBow Press
A Division of Thomas Nelson & Zondervan
1663 Liberty Drive
Bloomington, IN 47403
www.westbowpress.com
1 (866) 928-1240

Scripture taken from the King James Version of the Bible.

ISBN: 978-1-9736-7548-8 (sc)
ISBN: 978-1-9736-7547-1 (e)

Library of Congress Control Number: 2019920034

Print information available on the last page.

WestBow Press rev. date: 12/19/2019

Contents

To my grandchildren River, Kurtisha, and Kurt Jr.

Acknowledgments

I WOULD LIKE to acknowledge the contributions made to this book project by the following persons

Robert H. Thompson III MD
Ms LaDia Carrington Bachelor of Science in Computer Science
Mr. Shaheem Ross a positive young man

Thanks to these individuals for affording me the privilege of sharing part of your life experience.

Thanks to Ms. Cindy Van Wingerden, Ms. Nasha Mathurin, Ms. Janet Jeffers, Ms. Anna Martinez, for providing technical support.

To all family members, friends, coworkers, and well wishes who have encouraged me along the way. My husband Sullivan Seraphin, my friends Vanda Alezy Baptiste, Christopher Monbelly, Vivian Prince and Anette Henry.

Special thanks to my special friend Paulette Mason and my son Kurt James Sr. Both have been a source of practical support and overall encouragement from the inception of this project.

Preface

WHY THIS BOOK? Why another motivational book? Why not? I believe each book is unique in its own way. This one is the first in a two-book series.

This book explores some of the problem's teens and young adults face. It suggests possible solutions to some of those problems. Many of the suggestions are reinforced by true stories of real people, and how they coped with the difficulties they encountered daily. It encourages readers to rely on God and faith to cope with the daily realities of life. There are many references from the Bible. Like many others, I believe that the Bible is the greatest book ever written and contains the answers to any problem imaginable.

I have worked with children for three-quarters of my life, but for the past ten years, I have worked with teens who got in trouble with the law. Some are charged with simple misdemeanours, and others with more serious crimes, like grand larceny, and even murder. I am disturbed by the fact that many of these youths seem to have no dreams and little hope for the future. Sadly, many have little or no guidance. If this trend continues, I wonder what will become of the next generations of black males, especially black Caribbean, African American, and Hispanic males.

Young men—how many more of your fathers, brothers, uncles, nephews, friends, and acquaintances have to die before you realize that you are an endangered species on the verge of being extinct? You were born for a specific purpose. You may not know what that purpose is at this time but one thing is for sure, you were not born for a life of crime, violence, and hopelessness.

Young ladies—you were born for a specific purpose. It does not include being anyone's slave, property, or punching bag. The words of Jesus found in John 10:10 says: "I have come that they might have life and that they might have it more abundantly." **KJV** There is nothing abundant about killing each other, robbing from others, abusing others, or in revenge killings.

I believe words are powerful. The words "Hard work brings success" were first introduced to me in elementary school. One of my teachers wrote these words on the chalkboard for writing practice. I am not sure if these words were penned by her or by someone else, but I never forgot them. When I was in high school, I marvelled at my cousin whom I think of as my brother. We grew up together. He was always very smart, and he got good grades in school, although I never saw him studying as hard as I did. It was at that time that the words "Hard work brings success" became my personal motto.

Perhaps this is what made me decide to begin each chapter with inspirational words. The words are also intended to awaken interest in each chapter. The poem at the end of each chapter is intended to reinforce some of the ideas suggested. My hope is that this book will be a source of encouragement for you, to dream big and go after your dreams, regardless of your circumstances or the obstacles you may encounter along the way.

Realize that dreams do come true and miracles are happening daily. See disappointments and difficulties not as obstacles, but as learning experiences. The chapters are short and simply written for easy reading. Some people may not agree with some things suggested here. I do not claim to have all the answers for the problems of the youth today.

If any part of this book makes you think deeper about a particular topic, a seed has been planted. If any topic generates a discussion in any forum, germination has begun. If a discussion on any topic leads to some positive action, growth has begun. I would have achieved at least the first part of my objective for writing this book. Thoughts must be formulated, discussions done, ideas developed before any action can be taken, with the hope of producing a positive change.

So read, think, discuss, enjoy, and if possible, try to make some positive change in your life.

Introduction

IN THE EXUBERANCE and innocence of youth, life's difficulties, disappointments, and major problems seem distant. Stories of trouble and unfortunate circumstances are associated with other people. As we grow older and hopefully wiser, we will realize that both good and bad will touch our lives, either directly or indirectly.

Life can be likened to a journey on a road with potholes, rugged terrain, hairpin turns, high treacherous mountain passes with narrow uneven tracks, roads with no sidewalks, and highways with no shoulder to pull off in case of an emergency. There will be other times when the road on the journey of life will be smooth, wide, and even, with beautiful flowers on either side.

There will be times when the view from a mountaintop will be so picturesque it will take your breath away. The sunset will be so gorgeous it will seem almost spiritual. There will be times on the journey when we will pass through a valley so lush and green it will make our heart ache with pleasure. As we mature and grow older, we will realize three fundamental truths:

1. Everyone was born for a purpose.
2. Man was born with a void, an emptiness that longs to be filled.
3. How we fill this void will shape how our life evolves, whether or not we have a fulfilling life.

The people we encounter in our life, our experiences, the environment in which we grow up, and the choices we make will all influence our journey. If we make Jesus the center of our life, the journey will be meaningful. We will understand our life's purpose and the emptiness will be filled. We may not become rich and famous, or even successful by the world's standards, but nothing could compensate for the inner peace and contentment that comes with a relationship with God, through his son Jesus Christ. This peace comes from knowing that no matter what happens, you can be assured that all things will work for the better. Romans 8:29 reads, "And we know that all things work together for good to them that love God." **NKJV**

You are Special
Believe in Your
Ability to Succeed

*Believing that you can succeed in any endeavor is a
major part of actually succeeding.*

"YOU CAN DO it, just believe in yourself!" These are very
encouraging words that many will hear at some point in their life,
maybe several times during their lifetime.

A mother may say them to a child at different milestones in his life.
Perhaps he will hear this as he makes his first unsteady footsteps, or
as he gives his first stage performance. The words may be shouted by
adoring fans to someone on a sport field trying to accomplish a task
or win a game. The words may be said to encourage a disillusioned
student who wants to drop out of a class. A caregiver may say these
words to a senior citizen who is trying to learn a simple task all over
again after a serious illness. Believing in yourself however, could
be either a negative or a positive thing. What if you believe you
can't succeed at a particular thing? You probably won't. You can

1

only believe in your own positive ability if you have a good sense of self-worth.

SELF-ESTEEM

Your self-esteem may have been shaped by early life experiences. You may have been told from a small child that you "can't" so many times eventually you believe you really can't do anything. You may have been victimized or

Ridiculed many times in your younger life. You may have been teased or bullied because of your looks or for some other reason.

Real beauty. A person's real beauty comes from his values. This can be recognized by his actions and beliefs and how he impacts the world around him, not his physical appearance. The kindest most understanding and cooperative people in the world rarely fit society's profile of beauty. While outward appearance may be pleasing to the eyes, it is not a requirement for the most important things in life. It is not a requirement for serving God, getting a good education, or becoming a productive member of the society. Outward beauty will fade with time. Our good or bad name will be remembered long after we are gone.

Improving self-esteem. You can work to improve your own self-esteem. You must first believe this truth that you were born for a specific purpose. Regardless of the circumstances of your birth, it was no accident or mistake, but part of God's plan. Each morning, take a few minutes to engage in positive self-talk, as the younger generation would say, to "big up yourself." Say softly to yourself or in your mind, "I was born for a purpose. I am beautiful on the inside. I am worthwhile." Continue saying these words daily and eventually you will begin to believe them and your self-esteem will improve.

Help the less fortunate. Another way to truly feel better about yourself is to do something kind or special for someone else. There is just something within us that makes us feel wonderful when we help someone in need. Some of the most contented persons you can meet are some of those who work in an environment where they have an opportunity to be of service to others, or those who do volunteering work for the less fortunate.

As a student, you can do simple thoughtful things for your classmates. Some ideas are suggested in chapter 6. Many high schools require some community service hours to graduate. You can use this opportunity to volunteer at homeless shelters, soup kitchens, or senior citizens homes or centers.

Develop your special abilities. Each of us is born with special gifts or talents. If you think back to your earlier school days, you would remember someone in each class who was exceptionally talented at some specific thing. Some may have excelled in one of the traditional school subjects, or some other area such as singing, music, acting, art or public speaking. Someone may have been just good at fixing things. These special abilities are no accident, but part of a greater plan for our lives. You know yourself better than anyone else would know you. What positive thing interests you most? What are you really good at? Try to develop that special thing and be the best you can be at it. It could lead to your life's calling.

Don't allow anyone to put you down. Many children are teased or bullied in school every day for various reasons. This could be truly devastating to those children. It is even more so to those who already have a poor self-esteem. To them, school could be a nightmare instead of being some of the best times in a young person's life. The following is a true story of teasing and how one young teenage dealt with it.

~~~~~~~

In the 1960s, in an Eastern Caribbean country, a teenage young lady was constantly being teased in school because of her dark complexion. She was very puzzled and wondered why she was singled out, when there were many other children in the class and the entire school who had the same complexion as she had. After thinking about it, she realized that it was not so much about her complexion as it was the fact that she was viewed as an outsider. She was not born in the same area as the other children in the class. While most of them grew up together and went from grade to grade, she came to the school at the age of twelve years. She decided that even though they did not like her, she would find a way to get their respect. She loved to read and study. She decided she was going to be the best student in her class. She also made a great effort to get along with everyone. She studied hard and excelled in class. After a while, she became very popular, and the teasing stopped.

~~~~~~

Don't let anyone define you. Don't allow anyone to stereotype you because of your ethnic background, financial status, or for any other reason that might not be considered as "normal" as someone else. Perhaps no one from your family has been to college. This does not mean you cannot or should not try to go. The only person who can prevent you from going is you. If you have the ability and the inclination, you can go. Even if your parents do not have the financial means, you may qualify for scholarships or financial aid. You may be able to work part-time and go to college part-time. With the advancements in technology today, you do not even have to leave your home to attend a college or university. All you need is a computer or some other suitable electronic device.

Maybe some of your relatives have been or are in prison. There is nothing in your DNA that says you have to follow in their footsteps. You could use their experience to avoid making similar mistakes.

If you live in a neighborhood where crime is rampant, it does not mean that you must also engage in the same kind of behavior. You can become a positive productive member of the society, regardless of where you were born, or where you grew up.

There are many examples in real life, as well as in books and movies of people who overcame incredible odds and achieved their dreams. There are many older people around you who grew up in humble circumstances and are respectable, some very prominent individuals in our society today. You can emulate them.

A Closer Look

You look at him with a question
And you think, he is so different
You look, and then look away quickly
In your eyes he is different,
But in his eyes you are different
We are all different, yet the same.

We have different faces and races
But are we really that much different?
You hope, dream, laugh, and love
And hurt and cry just as he does
Your fears and cares are just as his are
You need love and care just as he does.

Look again at someone who seems different,
Then get past the look. He is like you
Except for the special part of him
The part that makes him who he is
And the special part of you
That makes you who you are.

Question for Reflection

What are some of the things that you think can contribute to poor self-esteem of an individual?

Establish Priorities for your Life

Choosing the right priorities is a major step in fulfilling your dreams and aspirations!

EVERYONE HAS PRIORITIES, although you may not realize it. Your priorities are the things you consider most important to you, and these take precedence over everything else in your life. As young children, our priorities are decided for us. When an individual is born, his basic needs of food, shelter, and safety are provided for him by his parents or guardians, or by the state or country in which he is born. As a child gets older, he begins to take a more active role in making choices for himself. As a teenager and young adult, the choices he makes will have a lasting effect on his life thereafter. It is therefore important to figure out your goals, establish your priorities and make sensible decisions early in life, to create a meaningful life for yourself in the future.

Faith. Relying on your own strength and ability for survival in this world is senseless. We may rely on family and friends, but they can only do what they can. We need the help of a higher power. We should rely on God for guidance and to be our source of strength if we are to survive the struggles and stress of everyday living. It does not mean we won't face challenges, but we will be able to face them knowing God will help us to survive.

Family. None of us got to choose our family, but no amount of wishing can change the fact that they are. Everyone should make it a priority to try to maintain a healthy relationship with family members. Petty differences, jealousy, and lack of forgiveness can tear a family apart, but in difficult times, they are often the ones to give us support. There are times when families have put aside past differences and come together in difficult times like sickness or death. There are also times when families have forgotten or neglected to keep in touch with other family members, and as a result could not get in contact when they needed to.

Health. Having a healthy body and mind is essential to live our lives to the fullest. If we do not have good health, we would not have the energy to pursue our dreams and aspirations. We should make an effort to ensure healthy living as a priority.

Education. In order to provide for our basic needs in life, it is imperative that we make education a priority. As young children, we do not understand the importance of going to school every day. As we get older, however, we realize that whatever we decide to do to make a living, we must have some form of at least basic education.

Goals. Many teenagers go through life aimlessly, without planning or thinking about the future. For many, instant gratification is all that matters. It is important to note that in the absence of a plan, there is a greater chance for mistakes. Some mistakes that are made early in life can shape the entire direction of a person's life. It might not always turn out negatively, but more often than not, it does. It must be noted, however, that it is not impossible to rebound from mistakes. Some of these bumps in the road may be all you need to slow you down and cause you to drive more carefully.

The following scenarios, which are entirely fictional, will depict situations that some young people can find themselves in if they do not take life seriously, and if they do not plan and prioritize. The scenarios will also demonstrate how being aware of the importance of planning, setting goals, and prioritizing can create a solid foundation for building a meaningful life. It must be noted that in each of these scenarios there is no guarantee that the person will achieve their dreams. Some may try their best to do everything right early in their lives, but may lose their focus and end up not reaching their full potential. There are some who may seem to be going down a wrong path, but may suddenly change their ways. They begin to work hard and achieve their dreams after all. These are fictional scenarios not based on any particular person.

Scenario I

John is a sixteen-year-old male who is attending a large school. He lives with his mother who works mostly at night. He hardly sees her. She is usually coming home from work in the morning just about the time he is leaving for school. He is not doing well in class, and he is not sure what he wants to do when he leaves school. He smokes marijuana occasionally and skips school sometimes. He needs to begin to think seriously about improving his grades, and what he intends to do for a living in the future.

Scenario II

DaReem is a seventeen-year-old male who is in the eleventh grade. He is an average student who usually gets a grade of C in most of his classes, but he gets an occasional B. He hopes to be a builder and to have his own construction company one day. He is studying hard to get his high school diploma. He smoked marijuana in the past, but after going to a juvenile detention center once and attending some of the programs there, he decided to quit smoking and stop other illegal activities. He decided that he wanted to be the kind of person his parents would be proud of. His buddies whom he hung out with in the past, are still smoking marijuana. His only interaction with them now is related to schoolwork. Now, he is involved in various after-school programs that keep him too busy to get involved in anything else. It's been hard at times for him, but he is trying to stay strong, and he is focusing on his dreams. The possibilities are great for him, as long as he remains focused.

Scenario III

June and Georgina are both eighteen years old. They are best friends. June is pregnant with her second child. She had her first child when she was in high school at the age of sixteen. She dropped out of school the following year. She had plans to complete high school, but the last two years were not easy for her. Now she is pregnant again. She is on welfare and receives child support from the father of her first child, but it is irregular since he does not work all the time. She should try to explore what social service programs can benefit her situation. She should also try to obtain her GED (General Educational Development Certificate).

Living just two blocks from June is her best friend Georgina. They started preschool together and went from grade to grade, never failing a grade and always making the honor roll. While June dropped out of school in the eleventh grade, her friend Georgina went on to twelfth grade and graduated with honors. She has a full scholarship to a very respectable college to study nursing. She seems to be on the right track.

Scenario IV

Jesse is a seventeen-year-old male who has been in and out of juvenile center for the past four years. He started using marijuana at the age of eleven. It was introduced to him by one of his family members. He dropped out of school at sixteen. He was in the ninth grade. He has not thought about the future lately.

He has become disillusioned by his parents' divorce. It was the last thing he expected to happen to his family. His priority right now is to be with his "homeboys" in the abandoned house up the road from his home. They mostly smoke marijuana, but at times, they have done things that he knew were illegal. He needs to take a serious look at this lifestyle. If he continues the path he is going, he may end up in prison or addicted to drugs. He should share his problems with someone who can get him some help. He needs counselling to help him cope with his parents' divorce.

Scenario V

Tony is a seventeen-year-old male who is a straight A student. He has never gotten in trouble with the law. He has clear-cut goals and priorities. He wants to be a correction officer. He knows it is imperative that he does not get a criminal record. He stays away from anything illegal. His priority is to complete high school and obtain his diploma.

He would then like to go to college and get at least an associate degree in Criminal Justice. He then plans to complete the practical training necessary to become a correction officer. He does not hang out much with his classmates anymore. He believes many of them are now on drugs. He has no intention of getting involved with drugs. He spends a lot of time with his family members now and a few close friends who have similar aspirations as his. They play sports in the backyard or board games, especially on the weekends. If he sticks to his beliefs and remains disciplined, he has a good chance of achieving his dreams.

Scenario VI

Fifteen-year-old Frances is very intelligent and mature for her age. She is in a juvenile detention center. She was convicted of a serious crime. She will be in the facility until she is nineteen years old and then released. She realizes that she cannot undo what is already done, but she hopes to learn from her mistakes, and try to make a better life for herself when she is released. She decided to use the time while she is in the facility to prepare for the GED which she hopes to take when she is released. She then wants to go to college to get a degree in social work. After getting her degree, she hopes to work with teens who commit crimes. She seems to genuinely want to change her life for the better. She may encounter other problems, but if she remains focused, she has a good chance of achieving her dreams.

Scenario VII

Juan is sixteen years old. He is in the tenth grade in high school. Last year, he got A's in all his classes. He thinks he might do something in computers, or perhaps be a mechanic. He has never been in trouble, but he occasionally gets into small squabbles at school. The reason being because he tries to defend his friends. He tried smoking marijuana about four months ago for the first time. He has used it several times since then. He did not do well in his last two tests. It seems to be getting a bit more difficult for him to concentrate these days. There are three factors that can compromise his ability to complete high school:

1. He is a follower.
2. He has no clear-cut goals or priorities currently.
3. His use of marijuana may be affecting his ability to concentrate.

Scenario VIII

Sarah is a seventeen-year-old female who is in the eleventh grade. She wants to be a teacher. She has clear-cut goals, and she knows who she is and what she wants.

She is a Christian. Her goals are to obtain a high school diploma, to go to college, and to obtain a bachelor's degree in education. She then hopes to get a job within the educational system in her city. She would like to get married after getting her degree. She believes that if it is God's plan for her, it will happen. She decides that sex and pregnancy are not options currently in her life. Abstinence is her choice based on her faith. If this young lady remains true to her beliefs, she is on the path to becoming a teacher and a positive productive member of society.

Scenario IX

Shawn is a twenty-year-old male who dropped out of school in the eighth grade. He had no future plans before leaving school, and still does not know what he wants to do for a living. He does what he calls hustling to get by. At times, he would cut the grass for his neighbors. Sometimes he would get a few days' work with a construction company. Most of the time, however, he does not work. He smokes marijuana regularly and just hangs out with the guys. His parents provide his meals daily. If he does not change his lifestyle, he may turn to a life of crime to survive.

Scenario X

Janice is an intelligent sixteen years old in the eleventh grade. She wants to be a nurse sometime in the future but has not thought about prioritizing or planning. She has a boyfriend with whom she is intimate sexually. She is presently pregnant and has had to drop out of school because her pregnancy has been difficult. She hopes to attend night school after the baby is born, if her mother agrees to babysit for a few hours in the evenings. She is stressed out and just wants the pregnancy to be over. It is not impossible for her to realize her dream of becoming a nurse, but she will have to be determined to succeed and make a plan. She will also need lots of support.

The following true story demonstrates how determination and family support can get you through in spite of challenging circumstances.

~~~~~~~

A TRUE STORY

About a decade ago, a very intelligent young lady got pregnant in her last year in high school. She graduated in the top ten of her class. This was out of a class of more than two hundred. She went on to college and got pregnant again. Four years later, however, she graduated with a bachelor's degree. She was summa cum laude of her class. This is truly a remarkable story of determination. She deserves a lot of credit for her achievements under the circumstances. It must be emphasized, however, that the key to her success, apart from her academic ability and determination, was the support she got. She had lots of support both emotionally and physically, not only from her family members but also from the family members of her partner.

If you live in the continental United States or one of its territories, there is a better chance of rebounding from setbacks or mistakes, especially if you are young. There are various programs that can help an individual in times of need or adversity. If you are under eighteen and you commit certain crimes, you are put in a juvenile detention center. With some exceptions, many records are sealed or erased at age nineteen. In many parts of the world, if a young person commits a crime, he may be put in the same facility and may be given the same punishment as an adult who commits a similar crime.

In most Caribbean countries, when a young lady gets pregnant in high school, she is expelled. Apart from the assistance she may get from her family and the father of her child and his family, she is on her own. The reality of the situation is that some young ladies become trapped in undesirable situations to survive. She may remain with the father of her child for financial support and possibly have another child even if any affectionate feeling between them may be over.

She may move on to a new relationship with someone who will financially support her and her child but will also want to have a child with her. Many end up with several children from multiple fathers. A few might decide to support themselves with several low paying jobs. Some might leave their children with their parents or some other family member and migrate to a different country in search of a better life. Pregnancy before completing high school is devastating to the Eastern Caribbean young lady.

In the United States, in the public school, if a young lady gets pregnant, she can choose to continue school until delivery, or if she prefers to return after. She can take advantage of different programs available to her that is especially created to facilitate and assist someone in her situation. There are programs that ensure that both she and her baby will get the best possible care to maintain good health. There are also programs to assist her to continue her education and try to put her life back on track. All fathers are bound by law to support their children in the United States.

Whether you are born an American citizen or naturalized, as a young person, you should try to take advantage of opportunities to better your life, even if you had a rough start. There are many people old and young throughout the world who would do anything to get a second chance in life. As Americans, you have a third, fourth, fifth, and sometimes sixth or more chances to make a positive change in your life. Make use of these opportunities; and remember, if you believe and trust God, nothing is impossible.

Life's Normal Progression

You would never have learned to walk
If you didn't first learn to crawl
You only learned to talk
After first learning to babble.

You would never have learned to read If
you didn't first learn your letters
You only learned to count
After first learning your numbers.

You can only live your best
If you take life seriously
And plan to live it well
With heavenly guidance daily.

Question for Reflection

Which of the ten scenarios touched you the most and why?

Dream Big! Set Goals! Work Hard!

Carefully mapping out your route will lead you in the right direction, even if you have to detour at times.

YOU HAVE EVERY reason to expect the best in life, and if you expect to succeed, you will. Your actions will reflect your beliefs. Success will not come by wishing and hoping. It will require planning, hard work, and determination on your part. Working hard for what you want is as relevant today as it was long ago.

Every child who is twelve years or older should have some milestones he wishes to achieve in the near future or sometime later. It may be a goal that is as simple as cleaning a closet, a room or passing a quiz or examination. Whether it is a simple short-term goal or long-term goal, the key to achieving is planning and implementing the plan. If a student has a goal to pass a quiz or test, he has to set aside a time to study, practice, or review. The time must be utilized wisely. There are more complex goals that would require a lot more time to complete, and more in-depth planning to achieve. You may need to plan mini goals that must be achieved before attaining the major goal. At times, it might be necessary to revisit or change certain parts of the plan, or even have the entire plan revamped.

Review your goals from time to time. You should write down your goals and review them occasionally; seeing them in writing will make them seem more real. It also allows you the opportunity to see exactly where you are in the process and your next step. A unique and very effective way was introduced to me when I entered college many years ago. On the first day after the formal orientation, the class was asked to write any essay on the following topics. Where did I come from? Where am I now? Where am I going? We were told that when we completed the essay, we were to give it to one of our professors. The essay was not to be graded. At that time, many of us didn't quite understand the reason. It became quite clear at the end of our two-year course. Where did I come from? This part of the essay was asking us to evaluate the journey that brought us to college. Where am I now? The question asked us to think of our purpose for being there. Where I am going? This last question was asking us how we planned to achieve our goal for being there.

On the last day, we were to evaluate whether or not we achieved our goal. Finally, we were to think about our plans for the future whether or not we wanted to continue to study. We learned a lot about ourselves by comparing both essays. It was a brilliant exercise that had a lasting effect on me.

As a young person, you could use this method as you enter high school. You can review your plans as you wish. Perhaps at the beginning and the end of each school year, or the beginning and the end of each semester. At this point in your life, you should know what subjects you need to improve or pay more attention to. For those subjects that need your attention, you should decide as soon as possible what you are going to do about them. Perhaps all you need to do is to pay more attention in class. You may need to read, study, or practice more. It this does not help, you could ask a teacher for help, or if your parents can afford it you can ask them to get extra help after school from a tutor. You cannot wait until the last week of the semester or the last semester of the school year to tackle the problem. It will be too late then.

Many adults are fascinated to hear young children talking about what they would like to be when they grow up. There are many who became exactly what they said they would be when they were only five or six years old. Then there are high school students who appear clueless. When asked what kind of job they would like to do when they grow up, they would shrug their shoulders and say, "I don't know." When questioned further, some admit they don't care as long as it involved making a lot of money. This is a very disturbing statement and poses a question, "Does this mean that they will be willing to do anything to get a lot of money even it is illegal?"

Understandable, not everyone will be exactly what they said they would be as a child. Childhood dreams could become unrealistic as you grow older.

A young child may dream of being a phlebotomist, but as he grows up still wanting his dream job, he realizes he faints at the sight of blood. Unless he overcomes this fear, it will be impossible for him to do this job. Can you imagine someone taking your blood and as they put the needle in your vein and the blood starts to collect in the tube, they faint? If this was not so dangerous it would be funny.

There is also the fact that many students enter college with the sole intention of studying for a particular profession. For various reasons they may eventually graduate in a completely different area.

Dream big. You should dream big as the saying goes "The sky is the limit." I do not know at what point in his life President Barack

Obama began to dream about becoming the President of the United States of America.

I believe that if as a child he had told some people that he had this dream, he would have been dismissed as having unrealistic childish dreams. Some may even have thought it was a funny joke. He however became President of the greatest nation in the world.

Don't let anyone discourage you from going after your dreams and aspirations. If you really want something and believe in your heart that this is the direction you should go, you are on your way to succeeding.

The next step is to be prepared to work hard and stay focused. A now prominent physician once told the story of his journey to become a doctor. He remembers it as though it was yesterday. He was in junior high school, and one day his class had some visitors. One of the visitors asked each student what they would like to be when they grow up. When it was his turn, he said that he wanted to be a doctor. The visitor said to him he should choose something else because he will never become a doctor. He said he began to second-guess himself. He was both puzzled and hurt because the visitor who told him he would never become a doctor was himself a doctor. He said that eventually he shrugged off his doubt and decided to prove the visitor wrong. He studied hard. Today, he is a capable, respectable, and caring physician in one of the most popular cities in the United States. He says there isn't a day he does not enjoy his job. He is happy he followed his dream.

He could have said to himself maybe that man is right and abandoned his dream. Instead it gave him the courage and determination to work harder to achieve it.

While it is important to plan goals and review them occasionally, and work hard to achieve them, it is most important to remember that

God has a plan for our lives. We should ask him to guide us to our true calling. Ignoring this will leave us as a ship without a sail, in the sea of life, being tossed about at the mercy of the wind and waves.

Believe

Life's journey could be disheartening
Ideas shattered as in a storm
There are times you wish you knew
The exact way for you to go
But if you trust God sincerely
And depend on his grace completely
The dreams you hold dearly
Will materialize for you surely.

Question for Reflection

What are some of your must passionate dreams currently? Are you actively working on any of them?

Take a Closer
Look at Education

Education is one of the main ingredients
in the recipe for a better life.

MANY PEOPLE ONLY consider certain jobs as being respectable and important. Not everyone can be a doctor, lawyer, nurse, teacher, policeman, secretary, a company executive, or a computer professional. These professions are important to any society, but so are skilled workers in the vocational trades. There will always be houses to build and repair, and other physical infrastructure in our communities to be maintained.

In some parts of the world, including the Caribbean, people are recognizing a shortage of skilled personnel like carpenters, masons, plumbers, electricians, tailors, and auto mechanics. There are quite a few people who have limited ability in these areas, but even less with advanced knowledge, skills, and abilities. If this trend continues, there might be a real problem in the next decade in many countries.

In the 1960s and 1970s, in parts of the Caribbean, many young people who did not go to high school learned a skill. The fact is at that time, fewer children attended high school or college. A form of apprenticeship was practiced. A young person should choose an area they like and would learn a skill from an employer in exchange for their labor until they obtained some competency in the particular skill. As they learned, they started getting a small amount of money, which increased as their skills increased. Some stayed with their employer and even took over the business when the employer retired. One of the negative aspects of this system was that some employers paid their protégé very little, even when their skills were greatly improved. Some also controlled how much their apprentices learned to prevent them from leaving for better opportunities. This form of apprenticeship is not very popular today and may not even be relevant.

Today, many more children attend high school, and many schools offer at least the basics in many of the skills. There are also many technical colleges in the US and at least one technical college in most Caribbean countries. Many young people do not take advantage of these opportunities. There are too many young people who do not complete high school and have no plans to try to obtain the equivalent certificate or learn a skill. There is another very important reason for learning a skill.

With the recent global economic downturn in countries around the world, many people have lost their jobs. Some companies, programs, and even hospitals and schools have closed. As a result, many workers were forced to retrain for different jobs. Having a skill is a head start to retraining.

The need for the basics. Don't fool yourself into believing otherwise, the academic basics are necessary. You need to be able to read and write legibly to do almost any job. A high school diploma should be the minimum expectation. A carpenter needs to be able to measure accurately to cut the wood he plans to work on. Likewise, the seamstress or tailor also needs to know how to read and measure to cut a material to sew.

The importance of reading. Any teacher will tell you that the child that likes to read gains a lot of knowledge generally. These children do well in most of the school subjects. As a young person, once you can read, you should read as many books as you can from your school library. There are many people who were self-taught exclusively by reading books. Some of these were famous people. One of American's founding fathers, Benjamin Franklin, was self- taught. Wikipedia.org on Benjamin Franklin states, "He had no formal education after age ten, yet he achieved so much in his lifetime. He was a leading author, printer, political theorist, politician, postmaster, scientist, musician, inventor, satirist, civic activist, statesman and diplomat." You may not realize the importance of being able to read now, but sometime in your life you will. Can you imagine having children and not being able to read them a story? Or having your child ask you as a parent "what does this word say", and you don't know what to tell them? You can also be easily victimized if you cannot read or write. Many have been tricked into signing away their rights to property and other important things. In most cases, if you cannot sign your name, you are asked to put an X to give consent for important documents. The problem is, if you cannot read, how do you know what you are putting your X to?

There is a folktale about a young man who could not read or write. He was about to travel to a foreign country to work. He told his younger half-brother to write a letter to the parents of a young lady he admired. He told his brother to let her parents know that when he returned in about two years' time, he wished to marry their daughter. When he returned two years later, he found the young lady already married to his brother. Had he been able to write, he would have written the letter himself.

Remember your dreams. If you find yourself out of school without a high school diploma, think seriously about your future. You may have once had a dream of how you wanted your life to turn out. Something may have happened along the way to put you off your track. You may not have applied yourself to your schoolwork or taken your education seriously. It might not have been entirely your fault. Perhaps you didn't have someone to supervise your homework or explain something you didn't quite understand. Maybe you are one of the children placed in special education and you were labelled as slow. The only problem may have been that you didn't grasp the basics in a particular subject. Just as it is difficult to build a strong house on a weak foundation, it is difficult to build on knowledge in a particular subject if the basics are not fully understood.

Whatever the reason is, you are where you are at this moment educationally. Don't use anything as an excuse or stumbling block not to improve yourself. Try to at least get your GED.

Do whatever you can to achieve that very important piece of paper. If this is not for you, try learning a skill. There are many who are not proficient in the academics but do great in a skill. Many have become very successful individuals in the community. Be honest with yourself. Recognize your strengths. Be realistic about your abilities. Remember you need to prepare yourself for a legitimate way of earning a living. Your quality of life depends on it. Now is the time to get serious. Reassess where you are, remember your dreams, and begin to work to achieve them, keeping in mind that knowledge is your ticket.

Educate

Enrich your life with knowledge
To meet life's many challenges
There is one sure way to manage
The chaos of each day's baggage.

Deduct from all you accumulate
That which will make you wiser
And if that includes college
Be sure to take the challenge.

Understanding is a major part
To open wide the door
To all the many choices
That life's opportunities may present.

Control youthful impatience
Take in as much as you can
Explore questions and engage
So you can ably evaluate.

Applying knowledge practically
That will be the greatest test
Of how much is absorbed
And what may apply functionally.

Turn your doubts and questions
Into positive productive answers
To make your life valuable
And meet its many challenges.

Empowerment is your ultimate goal
As you choose to embrace
A major principle of success
It's having a good education.

Question for Reflection

You have just graduated from high school, if you have a choice of a full 4 year scholarship to a college of your choice, or twenty thousand dollars in cash which would you choose? Why?

Say No to
Drugs and More

Since trying something once might be all it takes
to transform the entire direction of one's life, be
cautious of what you are about to try.

IN LIFE, MANY of us get involved with things that are not beneficial to us, and which may have far reaching consequences or irreversible effects on our entire life. At times, we may be aware of the potential danger, but get involved anyway. Sometimes we may not be aware of the danger. The young may be influenced by peers, lack of guidance, boredom, or just thoughtlessness. Whether you are old or young, you should think carefully before doing anything you might regret later in life. There are some things that everyone, especially the young, should be wary of.

Drugs. The young, in particular, should desist from using illegal drugs. The brain of the young is still developing. Research has shown that the use of drugs like marijuana and cocaine can impair the normal development of the brain. It is a fact that many of the people who get in trouble with the law are habitual drug users. Many early drug users are also school dropouts. Marijuana is sometimes thought of as a gateway drug, since many marijuana users later move on to more potent drugs. Many would say, "I'll try anything once," but once may be all it takes to lead to an addiction.

Alcohol. Alcohol abuse was once a problem seen in middle-aged and older adults, particularly males. Today, many more young men and women abuse alcohol as well. Like other addictive substances, once you become addicted, it is very difficult to turn that addiction around. Even when someone has completed a program for addiction and has been clean for some time, they are just one drink or one smoke away from the addict they once were. There are people who are in denial, and will say they don't have a problem, that they can stop anytime they wish. There may be a few who can, but most can't. Denial will be an obstacle to getting help. Until one admits that he has a problem, he is not going to seek help.

In some countries, people under the influence of drugs or alcohol cause more deaths through accidents than any other disease annually. The effect of death by impaired drivers can be totally devastating to the surviving family members. Many think these accidents were preventable. This may be the reason why, after many years, people still find it difficult to move on with their lives after losing a loved one because of an accident caused by someone under the influence of alcohol or drugs.

Guns. Everyone will agree that there is an absolute need for guns in today's society. Law enforcement officers need guns to carry out their job. Guns are also necessary for the men and women who defend their country in times of war, and for those who defend life and property on a daily basis.

Guns in the wrong hands can have devastating effects physically and emotionally. Every teenager either knows someone or has heard of someone who died senselessly by a gun. Every day throughout the world, someone is killed by a gun either intentionally or accidentally. Guns are the number one cause of death among the young in the United States. Every society has an obligation to keep guns away from those who should not have them. Adults in the home who own guns should secure them from children. Those in authority like lawmakers need to make it more difficult for children, the mentally challenged and the mentally disturbed to obtain guns.

One young man told me once that having a gun made him feel powerful and safe. In fact, the opposite is true. Having a gun as a young person makes you more vulnerable. You are more likely to kill someone or be killed by someone. If you get into a disagreement with someone, if that person suspects you have a gun, there is a potential for disaster. Both you and the other person will be thinking the same thing. "I must get him before he gets me." Your best option is to stay away from guns and circumstances that may result in you losing your life or taking the life of someone else. The Bible says in Proverbs 15:1, "A soft answer turns away wrath, but grievous words stir up anger." If someone speaks loudly to you in an argument, try speaking softly back to them. It surprises them because they expect you to try to be even louder and more forceful than they are. More often than not, the anger subsides. Try it—it really works. There are also times when you must walk away from situations. One young man said to me once, if he walked away from an argument or fight, he would be called a chicken. My answer to him was this question: "Which do you prefer to be, a free chicken or a fierce lion that is dead or imprisoned?"

Crime. Some young people get lured into illegal activities because of their love of money and power. Don't be coerced by the promise of a lot of money. Easy money is rarely legal. There is an adage that says, "If something sounds too good to be true, it probably is." Real power comes from realizing your purpose and living your life to the glory of God. It does not come by violence and intimidation.

Addiction may also lead to crime. Some addicts commit crimes to obtain money to maintain their habit. Nothing good comes from a life of crime. There are three possible outcomes: disability, imprisonment, or death.

Gangs. Gangs are closely linked to drugs, guns, and criminal activities. This is the nature of most gangs. If you are engaged in these activities, you are more likely to be attracted to or recruited by gangs. Think about it carefully. Being in a gang is a form of imprisonment. It is a life sentence. There are few people who get out of a gang and remain alive for long afterwards.

Sex. According to the teaching of the Bible, sex should be left for the proper and legal time and place. Apart from the moral aspect, there are other factors to be taken into consideration. Today, venereal diseases are rampant. Unplanned, unwanted pregnancies often lead to unfilled dreams and contribute to poverty.

Teasing. This may seem like harmless childish fun, but it could be very devastating to the young. If negative teasing continues, it can wreak havoc on the self-esteem of the young. There is an adage, "Sticks and stones will break my bones, but words will never harm me." While words will not break bones, it can break the spirit of an individual. This could be as devastating to individuals' well-being as sticks and stones to the body.

Bullying. This is one of the biggest problems in many schools today. Not only is there face-to-face bullying, but with the innovation of modern technology, there is cyber bullying. We have all heard news of young people who took their own lives because of constant, relentless bullying. There are many more instances of similar deaths than those that make the news.

If you were to look closely at the lives of many of the people who commit horrific crimes, you will discover that they were either abused, ridiculed, or bullied at some point in their lives. It is commendable that some schools have a zero-tolerance policy for bullying and teasing. This should be a policy for all schools or institutions that house young people.

Revenge. Many young people, especially young men, believe that if someone do them wrong, it is their duty to seek revenge at all cost. This belief has resulted in great loss of lives. If this trend continues, it makes one wonder what is going to happen to the next generation of black Caribbean African American and Hispanic males. Young men, how many more of your brothers, fathers, uncles, nephews, friends, and acquaintances must die before you realize that you are becoming an endangered species on the verge of being extinct? You were born for a specific purpose. You may not yet know what the purpose is, but one thing is for sure, you were not born for a life of crime, violence and hopelessness. For those of you who already have children, you are condemning your children to grow up fatherless. Some may never hear themselves be called dad or daddy. They may die before fathering a child. Then there are those who fathered a child but died violently before the child was born or while he was too young to understand.

To those children whose father died defending their country, you should be proud of the father you never knew. He died trying to make the world a safer place for everyone. But for those who died violently because of revenge or some other motive, it is sad and senseless. Let us be real, young people, revenge is not working. The cycle of killing and revenge killings may continue for a long time and over generations.

Try not to worry about taking revenge when someone does you wrong. Some people call it retribution. Some say "karma." Believers say leave it to God. Make no mistake, people who commit criminal acts and do horrific things to others will have to account for them one day in God's time and in his own way. The book of Romans 12:19 says, "Beloved do not avenge yourself, but rather give place to wrath; for it is written, 'Vengeance is mine, I will repay,' says the Lord." **NKJV**

Domestic violence. Young men treat your female companions with respect. Remember your mother is also a woman. I don't know many young men who would allow any man to hurt their mother or sister without trying to intervene in some way. Show the same compassion for all females, especially those you claim to love.

Young ladies be respectful and demand respect, and you will be treated likewise. You were not born to be anyone's slave or property. If a young man is showing interest in you and is overly possessive, don't just walk away run! If he wants to know everything you did in details when you were not with him—run! He has trust issues. Ninety-nine percent of the time, these kinds of relationships do not turn out well. If he hits you once and you believe it when he says it won't happen again, you are fooling only yourself. It will happen again and again. Domestic violence often results in severe injuries or death to either or both parties. Domestic violence occurs man to woman, and sometimes woman to man. Either way, it is wrong, and the outcome is the same.

Suicide. This is the third leading cause of death in teens in the United States. With regards to suicide in the Caribbean, in an article from informahealthcare.com, there are not many publications about suicide in the Caribbean.

The World Health Organization, in a publication dated June 2015, listed Guyana as No. 1 in suicide rates, not just in the Caribbean but in the world. Suriname was listed No. 5 in the world.

The fact is that many suicides can be prevented although there might not be much that can be done for those with mental problems. Many refuse to take their medications at a time when they may need it most.

As young people, it is important to remember what was discussed in chapter I. You were put on this Earth for a purpose. God wants you to be here. There are things that you as a teen can do to reduce the incidence of suicide in other teens and also try to prevent yourself from reaching the point of wanting to take your own life. If you are having any kind of problem, you must tell a trusted adult who will be able to get you some help. If you believe someone is thinking of suicide, or they tell you of their intention to do so, you need to encourage them to talk to someone. If they tell you they won't, then let them know that you will if they will not.

You should not tease, bully, or abuse anyone. You may contribute to driving them to suicide. Some people may be suffering from depression and are prescribed medications. The catch-22 is some medications which are prescribed for depression have side effects of suicidal thoughts.

There are also other medications that are prescribed for different ailments that have side effects of suicidal thoughts. If you are taking any medication for any purpose and you are having unusual or abnormal thoughts, it is best to see your doctor so that he may prescribe a different medication for your problem.

If you feel that you are in a situation that seems hopeless, know that your situation is not unique. You can be sure that somewhere in the world, there is someone who has been in a similar situation and has come out of it a better person. If everything seems hopeless or impossible, and it seems there is no one who understands, try reaching out to God in prayer. Talk to him as if he is right beside you. Tell him all the things you are ashamed of and ask him to help you through your difficulty. Believe he will and expect an answer to your prayers.

If you live in the United States and feel suicidal, and you need to speak to someone, you may call 1-800-273-8255. You can also call 911. Someone will get help for you. In the Caribbean, you can talk to a parent, a counselor, a pastor, or some other trusted individual who may be able to help you or get you the help you need.

Say No

Say no to drugs, no to tugs
No to things that bite like bugs
Say no to drugs.

Say no to booze, no to lose
No to things that blow your fuse
Say no to booze.

Say no to guns, they're no fun
Guns can put you on the run
Say not to guns.

Say no to crime, no to slime
No to things that make you do time
Say no to crime.

Say no to bullying, no to teasing
No to things that are not pleasing
Say no to bullying.

Say no to revenge, it's no defence
No to things that make no sense
Say no to revenge.

Say no to suicide, no to homicide
No to things that take a life
Say no to suicide.

Question for Reflection

Do you think as a young person owning a gun makes you safer? Why or why not?

Walk a Mile in Someone Else's Shoes

You can only truly understand if your experiences are similar.

WALKI NG IN SOMEONE else 's shoes literally could be very uncomfortable or impossible, unless the person has the same shoe size as your own. Even then, it could be difficult because everyone has unique feet. Criticizing another person's actions or reactions to a situation or incident is not sensible or fair if we have not had a similar experience ourselves. It is so easy to talk about what should or could have been done in hindsight. We should ask ourselves, "Had I been in a similar situation would I have reacted differently?"

The Golden Rule. The Bible says in St. Matthew 9:12, "Therefore all things whatsoever you would that man should do to you do even so to them, for this is the law and the prophets." **NKJV**

The world would be a better place if everyone would take this Bible verse seriously and make it a personal motto to live by. A very wise gentleman told me once that he was perceived as being too soft as a supervisor. He pointed out that it wasn't that he couldn't be firmer on others, but there was one important fact that affected how he supervised. He believed that he should treat others the way he wished to be treated. He felt that being harsh with someone might upset that person to the point that they might be unable to perceive what he really wanted them to see. He believed that it could get to an even worse scenario of putting a person's job in jeopardy. He preferred to try talking to the person to get him to correct the unproductive behavior.

Undesirable habits. There are some annoying habits that some people practice that may have serious effects on other people's lives. No one can sincerely say he likes to be teased, bullied, or called unkind names. Knowing that you dislike this practice and how it makes you feel; it is unfair to do this to anyone else. Another annoying habit is that of not waiting for your turn in a line. This may occur in a lunch line at school, but some adults also engage in this practice. Some people would just walk in front of someone in a line and take their place, totally ignoring the other person. Others might be subtle about it. They would come beside someone in a line and start up a conversation, then he would ask the person to do his transaction along with the person's own. The amazing thing is that people who would go in front of someone in a line are usually the same ones who would be angry enough to start a physical altercation if someone else ever tried to do the same thing to them.

Try not to talk unkindly about anyone. This is something almost everyone is guilty of at one time or the other. You may have had the experience of someone saying unkind things about you. You may remember how much it hurt. It may have been especially painful if what was said did not have a tiny bit of truth in it. Being mindful of this fact, we should refrain from talking unkindly or in a demeaning way about anyone.

Try not to judge others. Many of us are guilty of judging others daily. It is unfair to judge others. Most of the time, we do not even know the facts about the person or situation. Remember that a person is considered innocent until proven guilty. No one likes to be judged, so why should we judge others? The Bible warns us in Matthew 17:1-2, "Judge not that you be not judged. For with what judgment you judge, you will be judged, and with what measure you use, it will be measured back to you." **NKJV**

Be tolerant of other people's ideas. Most people have strong ideas about certain things. These ideas are usually developed from beliefs and experiences of the individual. Some people, however, are so opinionated that they believe only their opinion matters and anyone thinking differently is stupid or wrong. These people need to be reminded that, at least in most countries in the Western Hemisphere, freedom of speech is the law. Everyone is entitled to his own opinion. There are always pros and cons for every topic. It does not mean that a person is wrong or stupid if he has a different opinion. Many are so fanatical in their ideas and beliefs that they are ready to humiliate, hurt, or even kill others with opposing ideas. Many will argue that they are looking out for the rights of others, but they are forgetting that people whose ideas or beliefs are different from theirs also have rights.

Sympathize with others in their adversity or sorrow. Some people are not only happy when others meet difficulties, they would go out of their way to add to it if they could. This is especially so when they do not get along with that person. This is not something pleasant to do for several reasons. The book of Matthew 4:43-44 says, "You have heard it said 'you shall love your neighbors and hate your enemies,' but I say to you love your enemies, bless those who curse you and pray for those who spitefully use you and persecute you." **NKJV** Secondly, since none of us know what may happen in the future, we should try to do our best to sympathize with others. We may need their support, if we get in difficult circumstances.

Simple acts of kindness. There are some simple things that you can do for those you encounter daily, like your classmates or co-workers.

These are things you would appreciate someone do for you and expressing good manners and politeness. Almost everyone reacts positively to a smile. You can smile more to others. Also, you can give genuine compliments.

Most people would recognize a phony or half-hearted attempt at a compliment. As a student, you can share your snack with a friend or someone else that is in need. You may stand up for someone who is being victimized, bullied, or teased in class. You can help someone else to carry his books. You can try to discourage a fight from starting. If you are a senior in the upper grades you can think of more innovative things to do. If you see someone approaching a door and both hands are occupied, you can open the door for that person. Perhaps one of your classmates is having trouble with a particular subject that you do well, you could offer to study with that person. With the help of your teacher, you can do something really special for a well-deserving classmate. For this to be meaningful, it should be for a student who truly deserves it. Perhaps as a class, you can plan a birthday party for someone who never had one, or who is a really helpful, kind, and pleasant individual.

These simple acts of kindness would encourage others to do the same. A kind deed is like planting a small seed that grows into a huge tree that bears much fruit.

The things we do to or for others will come back to us, the bad as retribution, the good as blessings.

Before You Judge Men

Before you try to judge me
Come a while beside me
See the things I see each day
And hear the things I hear.

Before you try to judge me
Sit a while beside me
Talk and converse with me
And feel the things I feel.

Before you try to judge me
Walk a while beside me
Listen to my story
Before you criticize me.

Question for Reflection

What are some other acts of kindness that one can do as a teenager?

Recognizing and Managing Stressful Situations

Stress is one of the greatest destroyers of health and happiness.

SOME OF THE things that young people stress about appear to older adults as insignificant. For the young, however, it is real. Excess stress affects the health and well-being of individuals, and according to some experts, may be the root cause of many health problems. Young people can cut down on any type of stress by maintaining a good relationship with family members. It has been proven that when teens have a good relationship with parents and siblings, they are less likely to get into problems with the law. They are also less likely to abuse their own bodies or be involved in unlawful behavior. They may not want to disappoint their parents or some other close family members.

Teen stressors. It is important to recognize some of the factors that contribute to stress in teens and how to cope with or reduce stress.

➢ Poor self-esteem—many teens stress about some aspects of their physical appearance that they dislike. Self-loathing is closely linked to poor self-esteem. Some suggestions to improve self-esteem were discussed in chapter I.

➢ Home and family situations—there are many kinds of family situations in the home that can cause stress for teens. The sad thing is that the home is supposed to be a safe place for everyone, especially those who cannot take care of themselves. Whether the problem is an abuse of some kind, neglect, or poverty, there are solutions. As a teen, if you have a problem in the home, your best course of action is to talk it over with a trusted adult. Perhaps you could talk to a family member, school counselor, pastor, or teacher.

➢ Other relationships—some young teens seem to be in a hurry to get into a serious romantic relationship. The problem is that they may not be emotionally or psychologically ready for this kind of relationship. Many teens who get involved sexually at too young an age look back years later when they are older and think, "If I knew then what I know now I would have done things differently."— Richard Elder

➢ Peers—being accepted by peers is one of the most important things for many teens. It can therefore be a source of great stress. Suggestions on how to cope with peer pressure will be discussed in detail in chapter VIII.

➢ School work—not doing well in schoolwork can cause a lot of stress for teens. Many factors can affect one's ability to study. It is important to explore some of these factors.

  ▪ Health problems—you may be diagnosed with some form of behavioral development, psychological, or mental deficit, or other chronic health problem. The best you can do is to comply with your health professional's recommendations and take good care of yourself. You should do what you can so that you have the best life possible under the circumstances. If you are prescribed medication for a particular medical condition, you should take them. All medications have side effects, but if taking them will make you function better, the choice should be obvious. In my experience with cases of a psychological and behavioral nature, crises and problems are usually minimized if prescribed medication is taken as ordered.

- Disabilities—you may be a person who has had to live with disabilities of one kind or another, making it very difficult for you to do simple everyday tasks. Remember, it is not your fault that you have a disability. You were born for a purpose. If you are disabled because of an accident, blaming others will not help you grow to be all you could be. If you are living in the United States or its territories, there are laws specifically designed to provide you with access and assistance for your daily life.

- Poverty—many teens experience poverty daily. Not only do they stress about not having the necessities, they may also be experiencing hunger and unsafe living conditions. Poor nutrition can affect a person's ability to learn. If you attend school and know you are not getting adequate meals, you should utilize the meals provided by your school.

If you are not affected by any of these situations or problems, you have no excuse for not doing well in class. The key to doing well in schoolwork is paying attention as your teacher teaches. Don't be afraid to ask questions if you do not understand. Any conscientious teacher will tell you no question is a silly question as long as it is asked in a respectful manner, and it pertains to what is being discussed or taught. Sometimes in a class or gathering, a person would ask a question and others would snicker or even laugh, but among the people present there usually is at least one other person who would also like to know the answer to the question you asked. They may not have had the courage to ask. Don't ignore homework. The main purpose of homework is to practice and reinforce what was taught. Your teacher may also want to give you the opportunity to learn to research for information.

Never be a class clown. There are many intelligent students who have a sense of humor, but in my experience, I have found that most class clowns are not usually good students.

Stress relievers for teens:

> Sports—If you have the ability and opportunity, get involved in some sort of sports. Not only will it relieve stress, it will also be beneficial to your health physically. Your involvement in sports will keep you away from activities that might not be in your best interest.

> Pets—You can ask your parents' help to get you a pet of your choice. Pets are known to improve mental health and reduce stress. The time spent caring for a pet will take your mind off your own problems. Pets are good listeners, and they give unconditional love, something all humans crave.

> Music—A popular and very effective way to relax is by listening to music. Soft soothing music may be a choice to relax, or more upbeat type music may work well for other people. You should be mindful of the lyrics of some songs that glorify crime, violence, and immorality. You can learn to play a musical instrument yourself. The time and energy you devote to learning something new will take your mind off your own problems. A good opportunity to get to learn to play an instrument is by joining your school band, if your school has one.

> Books—Reading is a fun way to relieve stress, especially if you really enjoy reading. Through the pages of a book, you can be transported to exotic countries and enjoy exciting adventures. You can laugh at and cry with your favorite characters. This will make you forget your own trouble at least temporarily. You might be able to find a book that

can offer solutions for some of the things that might be troubling you.

Don't Stress

It's bad for the head
It's worse for the heart
Let it rest, don't stress.

It's bad for the mind
And worse for the spine
Let it rest, don't stress.

It's bad for the body
And worse for the soul
Let it rest, don't stress.

It's bad to be afraid
It's worse to worry
Let it rest, don't stress.

Question for Reflection

What are some other things one can do to help relieve stress?

Coping with
Peer Pressure

*No friendship is worth
compromising your moral beliefs.*

AS MANY PARENTS of teenagers know, peers can have more influence on teens than any other person or thing, in some cases more than parents. For some teens if they must choose between doing their parents bidding and what their peers want, the choice is obvious. They may choose their peers even if doing so will get them in trouble with their parents.

Generation gap. Teens may believe that their parents do not understand them, or that they are old-fashioned in their beliefs and thinking. This is especially true when it comes to moral values. The fact is that clothes and trends go out of fashion, certain things like morals and values never do. Belief in God, respect for self and others, truth and honesty—these things will always be relevant in every generation. The reason some youths are convinced that the values of the older generation are no longer relevant is because so many adults are engaged in behaviors that are hypocritical. However, this does not make these behaviors right.

As adults, we understand more than you think. We were teens ourselves and we still remember what it was like. We understand that one of the most important things for you as a teen is to be accepted by your peers. We understand that you want what most teenagers want, like fashionable clothes, name brand shoes, and the latest electronic gadgets. The fact is your parents have a hard time trying to provide for your daily needs and may not be able to also provide the extra things you want.

Legitimate ways to earn money for the things you want. You can do odd jobs for neighbors or friends for a fee. You may have a skill or hobby that has a potential financial benefit. You can see how you can use it to earn money. You can pack and carry out groceries for tips.

I had a discussion some time ago with a young man about the economic conditions in our community. He said something that I thought was very sensible. He said that at one time, he and some of his friends vowed they would never pack and carry out groceries as a part-time job. As he gets older, however, he sees it as a much better alternative to some of the criminal activities going on around him. I believe he is a smart thinking young man.

Hanging out with your own age group. It is human nature to want to hang out with others, with similar interests and age. The question is what do you do if everyone your age in your community is hanging out at the corner doing drugs and other unlawful activities? It may be difficult to resist, but if something is not going to be in your best interest, why get caught up in it? Many have gotten into trouble by hanging out with the wrong crowd. Some have gone to prison, when all they might have been guilty of is being there when the crime was committed. There is an old saying, "You are known by the company you keep." Even if you might not be doing wrong, if the people you associate with are, everyone assumes you are also. Innocent people have lost their lives by being in the wrong place, with the wrong crowd, at the wrong time.

If you know your peers are into trouble, you don't have to get involved, you can find other ways to occupy your time. Here are some suggestions:

- If you like sports, participate in some sporting activities.
- You can learn martial arts or some other skills. You can learn to play a musical instrument.
- If you are affiliated with a church, you could find out what youth programs you could be part of.
- Spend more time with family members. With your parents, you can plan a family night once a week, or when you wish. The entire family can play table games together.
- You can organize a movie night occasionally. With your parents'permission, you can invite other family members and some of yourfriends. You can all watch a movie together. Make sure the movie is one your parents will approve of. You can serve homemade popcorn.
- You may have feelings within you that you want to do something positive for your community. You can ask a family member, teacher, counselor, or church youth leader to help you organize a club or group to promote your cause.
- Another way to get away from being with the wrong people is to hang out with positive people who might be older than you are. There was a period of time when my son and some of his friends hung out with his uncles, t wo of my brothers, and a couple of their friends. This occurred even though there was a significant age difference between my brothers and his friends and my son and his friends. We never discussed it, but I know my son felt more comfortable and safer with them than some in his own age group. As a

mother, I also felt very comfortable knowing who he was out with. I have always felt grateful to my brothers and proud of my son's foresight.

Young adults and peer pressure. Many young adults are as affected by peer pressure as some teenagers. When they go off to college, they may engage in behavior they know is wrong. They may not want to appear different from their peers, so they allow themselves to be influenced by others.

Children of very strict or religious parents can be the ones most easily influenced. Many engage in the most outrageous behavior, usually the opposite of their parents' beliefs. Kudos should be given to those who stick to their beliefs, even with the possibility of being called strange, nerd, or other unflattering names.

In fairness to the youth of today, it must be noted that the influence of media in today's society is something that we as older adults did not have to contend with.

You are constantly bombarded by how you should or should not look to be considered beautiful and trendy. Try to keep in mind at this particular time in your life that it is more important to stay in school and get a good education than to be considered cool and trendy.

Wanting to be with your peers is normal. Being with them even when you are aware, they are engaging in illegal activities is foolish. Any affiliation, whether it be peers, clubs, organizations, gangs, or any other group that might jeopardize your life or the lives of those around you isn't worth it.

Any group that would require you to disobey your parents or compromise your personal beliefs and values is not worth your precious time.

Wanting to Belong

He was not mad, he was not bad
He was just a cool little lad
Who just wanted to belong.

So often he was present
But he was never unpleasant
He just wanted to belong.

He looked like the villain
But he was not the bad one
He just wanted to belong.

Just like that he was gone
Not because he did wrong
He just wanted to belong.

Question for Reflection

Your parents forbid you to invite your friends to the house when they are out. Your parents are away, and your best friend ask to come over. What would you do?

Supporting and Respecting a Parents Role

Unconditional love is
synonymouswith parenthood.

PARENTS TODAY HAVE a lot to contend with. Many are single parents and do not have the time or energy to be as involved as they would like to be in their children's life. It is a fact, however, that as children, your parents are responsible for you; and most, if not all, parents want the best for their children. You can help to make your parent's job easier by being a caring, thoughtful, and cooperative son or daughter.

Chores. Doing the chores is like a rite of passage for most children. More than any other person, you know your parents' likes and dislikes. A way of keeping a harmonious relationship between you and them is to avoid the things they dislike. You know they dislike coming home from work and finding dirty dishes in the kitchen. Then don't allow it to happen. You can do the dishes, even if it may not be your turn to do them. Chores are great teaching tools. When your parents demand that you keep your room clean, they are preparing you to keep your house clean when you have your own home.

When they ask you to prepare the supper once a week, it is not because they want to give you extra work to do. They are also giving you practice in cooking, a skill you will need in the future when you have a family of your own.

Rules and boundaries. Some conflict may arise from rules and boundaries set by parents or guardians. Teens want to be treated as adults in certain ways and as children in other ways. They would like to remind parents that they are only children when asked to help care for younger siblings. They would, however, like to be treated as an adult when it comes to having a curfew. They would like to come and go, to and from their home, whenever they wish. They should realize they cannot have it both ways.

Communication. It is important to talk with and listen to your parents. Let them know about certain issues and find out their feelings. It depends on the type of relationship between you, but as a child you should feel free to tell your parents almost anything. Many teenage problems like teen pregnancies, drug use, suicides, and gang-related activities may be reduced if teens would share their fears, concerns, and problems with their parents.

Needs versus wants. Young children make unreasonable demands on parents. They should be excused, but if you are a teenager, you should be able to understand the saying, "Money doesn't grow on trees." We must work for it. Another valuable lesson to be learned by teens is that in life, there are needs and wants. While you need food to live, you do not need an extra pair of name brand shoes to go to your friend's birthday party, especially when you have several pairs in your closet already.

Sacrifice. Parents regularly put aside their own personal needs for that of their children. If you think back, you may remember asking your parents for something and they may have told you that they did not have the money. Then sometime later, perhaps the same day, they gave you the money anyway. Have you ever wondered where or how did they get the money? They would not burden you with the truth, but perhaps it was money they were saving for something special for themselves or for the home.

Pleasant surprises. You can surprise your parents by doing simple but thoughtful things for them. Imagine you are a parent coming home from a long, hard day's work and finding a pleasant surprise. Maybe dinner is warming on the stove ready to be served. Perhaps it is the job you have been dreading for days, the load of laundry that you have been putting off, and it was done by your children. Any parent would be proud and happy to have children who are so thoughtful.

Older siblings. About four decades ago, the older siblings, especially the oldest child, had a huge part of the responsibility of helping to raise the younger children. At times, this may have negatively affected the older child. Many had to put the well-being of the family before their own needs. There are many older children who never completed elementary school. They may have had to stay at home to care for their younger brothers and sisters. In the absence of some fathers, many had to work to supplement the family income. Thankfully, at least in the Western world, this practice is no longer popular, although babysitting younger siblings occasionally is quite common. A much better role for older siblings would be a positive role model for younger family members. As an older brother or sister, you should realize that your younger siblings are watching and learning from you. Don't be responsible for introducing them to an undesirable lifestyle.

Your parents want the best for you. Don't assume that because your parent's lifestyle may not be what they wanted it to be that they want the same for you. Generally, all parents want their children to be better off than they were in every way possible. Your parents may be hard on you about certain things and you may become defensive and puzzled.

Perhaps you would like to ask them certain questions such as "How could you tell me don't do XYZ or that I must do A before B when you obviously did not follow the advice you are now giving to me?" The truth is, because they experienced problems or setbacks that resulted from their own actions and choices, they want you to avoid making similar mistakes. When your parents are encouraging you to stay in school and learn as much as you can, it is because they want you to be prepared to earn a decent living in the future. Maybe they did not complete high school themselves or were not exposed to the opportunities you have today. As a result, they may have to work two or three low-paying jobs to support the family.

You may not agree with some of your parents ideas, but you should respect them. The book of Ephesians 6:1-3 states, "Children obey your parents in the Lord for this is right. Honour thy father and mother (which is the first commandment with promise) that it may go well with thee, and thou may live long on the earth." **NKJV**

Parents

Providing for the family is expected
A generous helping of love included

Accepting you for who you are
That is the greatest gift

Respect is all they ask of you
In return for all they give

Encouragement is the glue
That keeps your life secure

Nothing is ever too difficult
For them to do for you

Turning frequent disappointments
Into huge, resounding successes

Systematically preparing you to face
An unknown future with grace

Question for Reflection

Name one thing you learned from your parents that you think will benefit you in the future.

Learn from Disappointments and Mistakes

What may sometimes appear to be mistakes
may be lessons of preparation.

AS LONG AS we are alive, disappointments and setbacks will touch our lives in some way. Some people may have horrific experiences, and may become angry or bitter wondering "Why did this happen to me?" As difficult as this is to believe, some good always results from something negative.

Some families of victims and sometimes victims themselves refuse to remain bitter; instead they turn their grief and pain into positive actions. As a result, there are many organizations formed out of their despair. These groups bring together people with similar experiences for much needed mutual support. They also change and implement laws to minimize and prevent similar occurrences. There are many who are alive today fulfilling their role in life because of the influence of one of these organizations and some of the laws they have helped to pass. The Amber alert is one such law that has saved the lives of many abducted young children. This gives credence to what many believe—it is not only what happens to us that determine the direction of our lives, but also how we respond to what happens.

Learn from the mistakes of others. You may be able to avoid some of the pitfalls of life by learning from the mistakes of others. The best people to learn from are our family members. Their stories will be more familiar to you. If you have a brother who either ended up in prison, or died young because of his lifestyle, you should try to avoid the same fate. You should ask yourself these questions:

1. What were the factors that led up to him being where he is today?
2. Do I want to end up this way?
3. How is it going to affect my parents if I follow in that person's footsteps?

Maybe you have a family member who became an addict or an alcoholic. How has that person's problems affected his lifestyle? Perhaps you have an older sibling who is struggling to support their home and family because of poor choices they made earlier in life. You should take a close look at the person's choices to see how you could avoid making similar mistakes.

Older, more experienced relatives are usually ready and willing to share their stories and advice with younger family members. Growing up, I got lots of advice from relatives. There is one person that resonates with me more than any other. It was somewhat out of character for this person. She was not in the habit of giving advice. It was the last time I spoke to my godmother or saw her alive. Even today, almost thirty years later, I still remember what she told me. She encouraged me to continue to go after my dreams, and to strive to be as independent as possible.

Coming to terms with your present situation. Perhaps you are a teenager between the ages of thirteen and nineteen, and you have committed a crime. You may be in a juvenile detention center in your city or state. You may be wearing an electronic bracelet and confined to your home. You may be on a 6 a.m. to 6 p.m. curfew. You may be on probation and have to complete community service hours, or you might be in an adult correctional facility because of the nature of your crime. Wherever you are, you can choose to spend the time positively or negatively. You can make plans to continue to do the same crimes that got you in trouble in the first place, or you may do the sensible thing. You can try to learn as much as possible from the programs offered to equip you for the real world after you have completed your time. You can take a long hard look at your life and how it is turning out. Is this the path you want your life to take? The persons you know or have heard of who started out as you did, where are they today? Do you know anyone your age that has died because of his lifestyle? Maybe you once had a dream or still do. If you continue on the same path, do you think you could still achieve your dream?

Steps to going about a change. You may be wondering how you could turn your life around. First and most important, you have to want to change for yourself, not for anyone else, or because someone else wants you to.

Having decided that you want to change, the next step is to reach out to people who can help you. You can reach out to family members, counselors, or any other person who will be a positive influence. You will need to prepare yourself for this journey. It will not be easy. You will have to be committed to the process and be prepared to make the sacrifices, but it can be done. Many troubled teens have turned their lives around, and some have even become counselors to troubled children. They are usually excellent counselors because their own history helps them to know exactly what these children are going through.

At this stage of your life, you are still a juvenile. In a few years, if you commit any serious crimes, you will go to prison and will have a permanent record of being a felon. Now is the time to take a serious look at your lifestyle and take steps to improve it.

To the teens and twenty "something" trying their very best to do what is right, kudos to you for being strong! Your parents, guardians, and teachers are very proud of you, even though they may not tell you often.

Realize that you are a positive example to many of your peers. Continue to be a beacon in your world and resist undesirable behavior.

Many of you will become the leaders in your community. It is important that you keep this in mind, as you prepare yourself to take over from the present generation.

Don't Give Up

Mistakes in life are inevitable
Not encountering any impossible
Disappointment, pitfalls, setbacks too
Are elements of the tests of life.

So, don't give up in difficult times When things
appear unimaginable This is just a part of life
That's all, but seems improbable

Problems are like puzzles to be solved
And lessons to be learned
And credits to be earned
For passing the tests of life

Question for Reflection

Have you ever done something you are not proud of and regretted it? Did you learn anything from the experience?

Reality Check

*As children we may have enjoyed, and even believed
some fairy tales. As we grow older we realize that
life can be wonderful, but it is no fairy tale.*

YOUNG PEOPLE TODAY are very intelligent and seem to be wise beyond their years, especially with the use of technology. As youths, you know more about how to operate electronic gadgets than many older people do. There are areas in life, however, in which some youth appear to see things in a way that might not be realistic. This could cause problems or hardships in the future.

Emulating those who seem to have it all. The lives of some celebrities seem so glamorous and fascinating on the surface. It may be difficult for anyone to imagine the not-so-glamorous side.

Entertainers, TV personalities, models—while there are quite a few stars in Holly wood who appear on television, radio, or in popular magazines, there are only a few rags to riches stories. Not many can boast of going to Hollywood, Paris, or London, with only a few dollars to their name and then become very successful. There are not many who know someone who can help to jump-start their career in the entertainment field. If you live in a small state or on an island, the reality is you may not be able to adequately support yourself as a singer, musician, model, or entertainer. It will be a good idea to have a backup plan or a supplementary income.

- Paid athletes—some paid athletes and other sports personalities seem to have a truly wonderful life. As youths you may wish you could have the life they have. As glamorous as their life may seem, sports personalities must perform well at all times or they can lose their benefits. Sometimes minorities and others realize that being exceptionally good at the sport of their choice could be their ticket out of poverty or to a more affluent lifestyle. The reality is only a small amount of these actually succeed in getting these opportunities. There are also not many countries or organizations that can afford to pay their athletes a lot of money.

Another thing to take into consideration is the fact that the careers of sportsmen, models and some other entertainers are often age-limited. There are not many models over the age of twenty-five, and not many athletes over the age of thirty-five who are able to continue to function at peak performance.

The lesson here is if you really want this type of future, to represent your country or state in sport or arts, strive to be exceptionally good at what you do. Don't give up your dreams. Continue to work toward them, but also be sure to prepare yourself in case things do not work out as planned.

The way to prepare yourself is by taking advantage of your educational opportunities. Get your high school diploma. If possible, earn a degree at college, learn a skill, or start your own business enterprise. Many young people today who go to college realize that the job market can be unpredictable, so instead of just concentrating on one area of major studies, they choose to incorporate some minor studies. After graduation, if they did not get the job in the field they wanted, they would turn to an area of minor studies. Even some stars think ahead and get a college degree or start a business, because they realize the unpredictability of the entertainment field.

Looking like your idol. It is very important for some youths, especially young females, to look like the people they admire and see on television or in magazines. Problems may arise because some young people would do anything, including starving themselves, to look like their idols. This may result in not consuming vital nutrients or developing eating disorders such as anorexia or bulimia.

Then there are those who find themselves using food to cope with stress. They may eat when stressed and put weight on, which then creates more stress, and it becomes a vicious cycle for them. This revolving door effect can lead to other health problems including obesity and diabetes. Another factor that can affect eating habits is the confusion about which foods are healthy and which are not. Guidelines are constantly changing. Many of these changes are announced after some study by some prestigious organization or group of health professionals. Some food items that were considered healthy at one time might have been deemed not so healthy after one such study. A smart guideline to follow is to eat a variety of foods, paying special attention to portion control.

A different lifestyle. With the availability of technology today, future generations will be at risk to have more sedentary lifestyles than previous generations. When their parents were growing up they enjoyed playing some sort of ballgame in their front or backyard. Today, however, many youths prefer to be surfing the internet on the computer, texting with friends or listening to music on their device.

They may be missing out on much needed exercise. Adding to this is the fact that young people today do a lot less walking than previous generations tended to do.

As a student, if you are not involved in some sporting activity, you should try not to skip your gym classes. The exercise will be beneficial to your overall health. If you are older, you should try to get involved in some structured exercise program. It could be as simple as walking.

Money and material possessions. Everyone needs money to live, but we should not be too obsessed with it. Anything that money can buy can be destroyed in an instant. Most importantly, money cannot buy happiness or eternal life. Money is not usually easily obtained. A few people do earn money from a lottery or gambling, but few people know someone who has won a lot of money. The reality is we are more likely to get struck by lightning than to win a lot of money. There is one way to legitimately get money and that is to work for it. While material possessions can be convenient, you can't take them with you when you die. A question worth exploring is, "Why do we work so hard to acquire so many things when we cannot take anything with us when we die?"

Addiction. Young and not-so-young people may say, "I am not addicted. I can stop smoking or drinking anytime I want to." The truth is, if they could do it on their own, they would already have done so. Addiction is no simple matter.

It is a chronic disease that must be treated and managed for the rest of one's life.

Growing up can be exciting, but for some it can be very difficult. Children can be victims of circumstances over which they have little or no control. If your life fits this profile, try not to be bitter and indulge in self-pity and un-forgiveness. These emotions can make you stuck, revengeful, and unable to move forward in your life. If you need help, get help. Find a counselor or pastor who will help you process your pain.

Remember what was discussed in chapter I and touched on in several other chapters? You were born for a specific purpose. While some seem to know their purpose by the time, they can write their name, others take a much longer time to find out. Try to discover yours. Life will become more meaningful.

If you are a teenager on the verge of adulthood, this should be one of the best times in your life. It should be an exciting time to be alive. Your life is before you like an empty canvas. You are the artist who will turn that canvas into a picture. Give it a lot of thought. Plan carefully. Choose your colors wisely. The picture you are creating will be your future. Create a masterpiece!

Name one person you admire. Why? It could be someone you have heard of or someone you have met.

Adulthood

Part of the responsibility of a grown up is realising that apart from God each of us is liable for our own wellbeing.

YOU ARE ALMOST over those troubled teen years, or maybe for you they were not so troubled at all, now what? It is exciting to be of legal age to be able to do certain things, but one must realize, with more privileges comes more responsibilities.

An entitlement culture:
The present generation seem to have more of a feeling of entitlement than previous generation had. One can hardly blame them since this feeling seem to be reinforced by some of the things that our society does. Social promotion is still being practice in the U.S and other parts of the world. As a result, many students are not motivated to study, since they know they will be promoted to the next grade whether or not they pass their final exam. There is an even deeper message here; it is that one may not need to work hard for anything, since he might get what he wants anyway.

This is also generation of instant gratification. With the development of social media, and reality television today, we see how easily some people get catapulted to fame and fortune almost overnight. One can understand how some young impressionable minds can easily believe "this could be me." Be honest and realistic, think about where you are in your life at the present time. Ask yourself the question how likely is it that I could be one of those persons? If you are honest with yourself the answer should be clear.

Self-Reliance:
You are setting yourself up for disappointment and failure if you believe you are entitled to certain privileges and benefits in life, or that it is easy for anyone to become successful or wealthy overnight, as is often seen on television. As adults we are responsible for our own well-being. We should be prepared to work hard to fulfil our individual dreams and aspirations.

It is important to note that self-reliance does not mean one should not accept assistance from others. As a Christian I believe God puts certain people and circumstances in out path during our lifetime to assist us.

There are many young folks today who have planned and are working very hard and taking advantage of all opportunities available to them, to prepare and advance their lives. There are however, too many young men of color, who desire the finer things in life, but are not prepared to work hard or sacrifice to get them. As a result, some engaged in illegal activities to survive. It is a fact that some young men will prefer not to work at all, than for minimum wage; even if the job they are asked to perform, either require no skill, or skills which they do not possess.

There are also too many young ladies who depend on some government programs to survive, instead of trying to support themselves. This is especially true for those who have young children and receive little financial support from their fathers. Some of these young ladies become trapped in a life of dependence on some of these programs.

There are some instances when government assistance can be just what is needed to get out of difficult situations. Think of the young lady who is a high school dropout and a single parent who wants to improve her life but has no other means to help herself. She can make use of some of these resources while she prepares herself for a job and a better living for herself and her child.

As a young adult there is one truth many might not be willing to admit to you, it is that at times, when faced with making difficult decisions, we as older adults ask ourselves the question, "Why was I so happy to be a grown up, when so much responsibilities come with adulthood? The Question is easily answered by just thinking about the benefits we experience daily. It is an inevitable stage of life we must go through if we live long enough. The secret is to try to be as prepared as one can be. While there is no blueprint to follow, or examination to pass, there are some things we can do to prepare ourselves for the inescapable transition to adulthood.

Helpful tips to prepare for the next stage of your life:

- Seek a relationship with God, life will become much more meaningful.
- Know who you are and strive to become a better person in every way.
- Try to obtain at least a high school diploma and/or a skill.
- Know what your plans are for the next two years, for example; Where you hope to live? Are you going to work or study?
- Continue to dream and work hard for a successful culmination of your dreams.
- Forget the feeling of entitlement, it will make you arrogant and a failure.

- Accept any reasonable, legal assistance you can get to make
  your life better but be prepared to work for what you want.
  Remember no one owes you anything. It was Mark Twain,
  pen name of the great American writer Samuel Longhorn
  Clemens, who said "Don't go around saying the world owes
  you a living. The world owes you nothing. It was here first."
  Mark Twain.

Printed in the United States
By Bookmasters